Spotter's Guide to
AQUARIUM FISHES

A guide to freshwater aquarium fishes

David Ford
Head of the Aquarium Laboratory at the
Animal Studies Centre, Waltham-on-the-Wolds

Illustrated by Sam Peffer and Annabel Milne & Peter Stebbing

with additional illustrations by
Andy Martin

Contents

Illustrations on pages 7 to 25 inclusive by Annabel Milne & Peter Stebbing; title page illustration and illustrations on pages 26 to 48 inclusive by Sam Peffer.

Designed and edited by Felicity Mansfield

Series editor Bridget Gibbs

First published in 1980 by Usborne Publishing Limited, 20 Garrick Street, London WC2

© 1980 Usborne Publishing Limited

Published in Australia by Rigby Publishing Ltd., Adelaide, Sydney, Melbourne, Brisbane.

Printed and bound in Great Britain by Morrison & Gibb Ltd, London and Edinburgh.

How to use this book

This book is a guide to popular freshwater aquarium fishes, and includes tropical fishes (which need a heated tank) and goldfishes. The other major group of aquarium fishes is marine fishes, but these are not dealt with in this book.

The first section is designed to help you identify the different species (types or kinds of fishes) and to help you select suitable fishes for your aquarium. The second section of the book tells you how to set up and maintain an aquarium of freshwater fishes.

Size
The descriptions next to the illustrations give the size that a good adult fish should be. Aquarium fishes are measured from the tip of the head to the end of the body. Many exotic new varieties have very long tails, so the tail· is not included in the measurement.

Countries of origin
The descriptions also tell you where the fish originally came from.

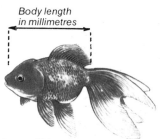

Body length in millimetres

Most of the species in this book came from lakes, pools and rivers in places like South America and the Far East. Many have now been bred into new varieties very different from their wild ancestors. Some fishes are difficult or impossible to breed in captivity; the only specimens you will see are wild ones imported from their natural habitat.

Males and females
Male and·female fishes of the same species are usually hard to tell apart, but occasionally there are marked differences, and these are pointed out in the illustrations.

Spotting fishes
Take this book with you when you visit petshops, public aquaria or exhibitions or shows held by aquarium societies. When you identify a fish, tick the blank circle next to the correct illustration. The scorecard at the back of the book gives a score for each fish you spot. A rare species scores 25 points, a common one 5 points.

Fish families

The names of fishes given in this book are the fishes' common, popular names. Because these names vary from country to country, scientists give aquarium fishes proper names, in Latin, to avoid confusion (see page 59).

Most proper names are made up of two words. For example, the Tiger Barb's Latin name is *Barbus tetrazona*. The first word is the name of the genus (plural: genera), the group of related species to which the fish belongs. The second word shows which species the fish is. Fishes of the same species look alike and can breed with each other.

Each genus belongs to a larger group, called a family. The Barbus genus, for example, belongs to the Cyprinid family.

The first part of the book is divided into sections covering the major fish families; the final section of the book (pages 41-48) illustrates some species that belong to the smaller families of fishes.

The most common families of freshwater aquarium fishes

1. Characins (pages 7-14). This is a Neon Tetra.

2. Cyprinids (pages 15-20). This is a Tiger Barb. (Note: Goldfishes are descended from coldwater Cyprinids.)

3. Cichlids (pages 28-33). This is an Angelfish, the most popular of all aquarium fishes.

4. Livebearing Toothcarps (pages 21-23). These are Guppies.

When you are looking for freshwater aquarium fishes, the ones you will most commonly see will probably belong to one of the four major families. Examples of each of these families are shown above. There is a great range of size and shape within each family.

The fish's body

A fish's body is designed to let it move easily through water. Most fishes have a streamlined shape, and flexible scales. They are covered in a protective layer of waterproof mucus (slime). Fishes swim using their body and fins. There is a gas bubble deep inside them which helps to stop them sinking in the water.

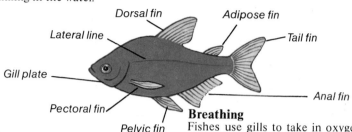

Dorsal fin
Adipose fin
Lateral line
Tail fin
Gill plate
Anal fin
Pectoral fin
Pelvic fin

Senses
In general, fishes have good, all-round vision and are quick to spot movement. They seem to be able to detect colours, too. Fishes have a very good sense of taste and smell. Some fishes have extra sense organs in the head, lips and barbels (feelers near the mouth).

Breathing
Fishes use gills to take in oxygen dissolved in the water. Their gills are covered by gill plates.

Lateral line
Fishes have a row of sensitive cells along the side of the body called a lateral line. The lateral line acts as a sort of radar, picking up vibrations in the water. This helps fishes to navigate.

You can find out quite a lot about a fish's natural habitat or behaviour by looking at its shape.

▲ Fishes that live among dense water plants are often tall and thin, like these Angelfishes.

▲ Fierce predators, such as Piranhas, have big, powerful jaws and lots of sharp teeth, used for biting flesh.

▲ The flat belly and downturned mouth of this Catfish show you that it feeds near the bottom.

▲ Surface feeders have flat backs and upturned mouths. They snatch insects that fall on the water.

5

Colouring

Wild freshwater fishes tend not to be colourful because bright colours attract predators. Some aquarium-bred fishes are so vividly coloured that they would not last long in the wild.

Male fishes are usually much more colourful than the females. Their colours may change or become even brighter during the breeding season, when they want to attract a mate. Distinctive colouring can help the young fry to recognize their parents, too.

Colouring may camouflage a fish, making it blend into its surroundings, or it may confuse predators by disguising or breaking up the fish's true shape.

Counter shading is a common form of camouflage, where the fish's belly and sides are lighter than its back. This offsets the effect of sunlight from above and makes the fish seem a flat, uniform shape, very difficult for predators to distinguish clearly.

Fishes change colour slightly when they are ill, and they become paler when frightened. Some fishes, such as Pencilfishes, have a different colour pattern at night.

▲ The Giant Gourami's stripes blend well with the plants around it.

Dark belly

▲ Counter shading is reversed on this Catfish. It swims upside down.

Eye spot

▲ The spot on this Festive Cichlid's tail looks like an eye, a point predators aim for. A fish can escape an attack to the tail more easily than one to the head.

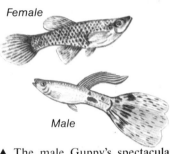

Female

Male

▲ The male Guppy's spectacular colouring and courtship display are designed to attract the drabber-looking female.

No eyes

▲ The Blind Cave Fish is a plain flesh colour. Because is it blind and lives in dark underground waters, it does not need distinctive colours or markings.

Characins

Characins (pages 7-14) come from Mexico, Panama, Texas, USA, and Africa. Characins (Latin family name: *Characidae*) have no barbels. The fishes on this page belong to three different genera of Characins.

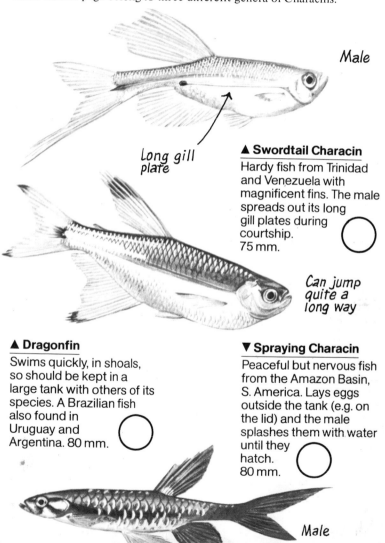

Male

Long gill plate

▲ Swordtail Characin
Hardy fish from Trinidad and Venezuela with magnificent fins. The male spreads out its long gill plates during courtship.
75 mm.

Can jump quite a long way

▲ Dragonfin
Swims quickly, in shoals, so should be kept in a large tank with others of its species. A Brazilian fish also found in Uruguay and Argentina. 80 mm.

▼ Spraying Characin
Peaceful but nervous fish from the Amazon Basin, S. America. Lays eggs outside the tank (e.g. on the lid) and the male splashes them with water until they hatch.
80 mm.

Male

Tetras

Tetras (pages 8-14) are good Characins for a beginner to keep, as they are generally peaceful and undemanding. Tetras have flat-sided bodies.

Has no eyes

◀ Blind Cave Fish
Lives in dark underground lakes in Mexico, and has no eyes. Navigates using its sensitive lateral line. Continually looks for food on the bottom.
Up to 90 mm.

Bloodfin ▶
An active swimmer, best kept in small groups in community tanks. Swims in shoals. Comes from Brazil, but many are bred in aquaria.
60 mm.

Fins are blood-red

◀ Buenos Aires Tetra
Originally came from the River Plate Basin in Argentina. Can live in quite cool water. Likes green plants and may nibble plants in the tank.
75 mm.

Dark, lozenge-shaped mark

Tetras

▲ Beacon Fish or Head-and-tail-light Tetra

Name comes from its red eye and the bright dot near the tail. Popular fish from the Amazon Basin. Easy to breed in the aquarium. 45 mm.

▼ Glowlight Tetra

Found in the shady jungle waters of Guyana. Also bred in large numbers in captivity. Named after the vivid red stripe on its side. Hardy. 45 mm.

Stripes look a bit like the French flag

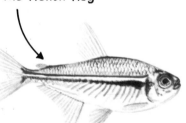

◄ Flag Tetra

Shy, rather delicate fish from the Amazon region, S. America. Should be kept in shoals of six or more. Prefers soft, acidic water. 50 mm.

Red-nosed Tetra ►

Another fairly shy fish from the Amazon region. The male is much slimmer than the female, but both have a red nose. Best kept in small shoals. 55 mm.

Male

Tetras

Jewel Tetra ▶

Comes from streams in Paraguay. Only happy when living in shoals. Its colours become very bright if it is kept in fairly soft, acidic water. 45 mm.

Sickle - shaped black patch

Female

◀ Griem's Tetra

At breeding time its body has a coppery glow. Can tolerate most types of water. Its natural homes are slow streams and still waters in Brazil. 32 mm.

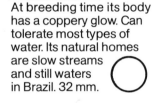

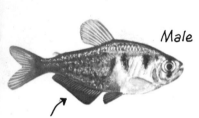

Male

Black edge

◀ Flame Tetra

A bright orange-red fish from the same region as the Griem's Tetra (its shape is similar, too). Hardy and easy for beginners to keep. 45 mm.

Lemon Tetra ▶

Translucent yellow fish from the Amazon region, S. America. Popular choice for community tanks because it is peaceful and hardy; but it is difficult to breed. 50 mm.

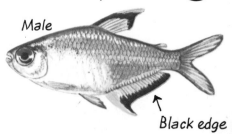

Male

Black edge

Tetras

◀ Black Neon Tetra
A typical Brazilian Tetra. The male is smaller than the female. Quiet. Only happy if kept in shoals of at least six. 45 mm.

Neon Tetra ▶
Very popular fish for a community tank. Now bred by the million in Hong Kong, but originally came from the Amazon, S. America. Likes soft water. 45 mm.

Cardinal Tetra ▶
Also comes from the Amazon. Very similar to the Neon Tetra, but more difficult to breed, so it is more expensive and a little less likely to be seen in aquaria. 50 mm.

The Neon Tetra has a shorter red flash

◀ Black-line Tetra
An ideal aquarium fish because it is easy to breed and well-behaved, but it is not particularly colourful. Swims in lively shoals. From the Amazon region. 50 mm.

Tetras

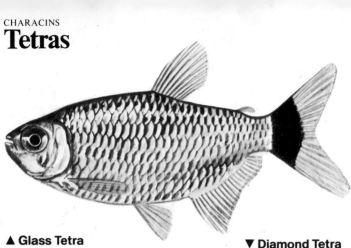

▲ Glass Tetra
Found in Guyana and the Amazon region. Small and colourless when young, but grows very large and may eat both the smaller fishes and the plants in the aquarium. 120 mm.

▼ Diamond Tetra
Peaceful fish from Lake Valencia in Venezuela. The scales sparkle in the light. Prefers to live in soft, acidic water. 65 mm.

The female is duller- coloured

Male

◄ Emperor Tetra
Popular Colombian fish now bred in fish farms for the aquarium. Usually peaceful, although the males sometimes behave aggressively towards each other. 60 mm.

Iridescent purple in bright light

12

Tetras

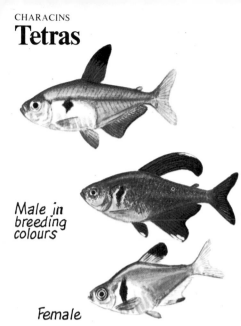

Male in breeding colours

Female

◀ Red Phantom Tetra

Fairly rare because it is not easy to breed in captivity. Its natural home is Brazil. Prefers living in shoals. Usually not aggressive. 40 mm.

◀ Black Phantom Tetra

Similar to the Red Phantom Tetra and also comes from Brazil. Easy to keep. Female is pale and reddish, male is black, except at breeding time. 40 mm.

X-ray Fish ▶

Found in most parts of northern S. America. Good, active aquarium fish. Prefers to live in large shoals. Body is translucent, not completely transparent. 45 mm.

▼ Silver or Platinum Tetra

Lively fish that needs lots of swimming space. The tank must be covered to stop it jumping out, too. Originally came from Panama. 65 mm.

Female

Female (Shape of males' fins is different)

Tetras, Piranhas

Penguin Fish ▶
Name comes from its
black and silver colouring
and its tilted, head-up
swimming position. Comes
from the Upper Amazon,
S. America. Lively
and well-behaved.
65 mm.

Male

▲ Congo Tetra
Needs a large tank with
plenty of swimming space.
Only the male has the long,
attractive fins. Named after
its native home: the River
Congo Basin
in Africa.
90 mm.

▼ Piranhas
All Piranhas come from
S. America. They have
sharp teeth and powerful
jaws. The Piranha and the
Red Piranha are very
dangerous. They can tear
off fishes' and other
animals' flesh in seconds.
Occasionally seen in
captivity, but always on
their own.
300 mm.

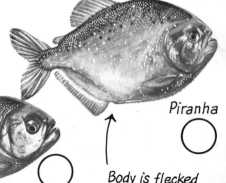

Piranha

Red Piranha

*Body is flecked
with shiny specks*

Cyprinids

Cyprinids (pages 15-20) are found all over the world. Cyprinids (Latin family name: *Cyprinidae*) have no teeth. They grind up their food using bony plates in their throats. The "Sharks" on this page are not true Sharks; they belong to one genus of Cyprinids. The Flying Fox belongs to a different genus.

▶ Flying Fox

Has not been bred in captivity, so specimens are all caught in Borneo and Sumatra, their native homes. Needs lots of space. Useful, eats algae. 140 mm.

Protruding snout ↗

▲ Red-tailed Black Shark

Comes from Thailand. Defends its territory fiercely against other fishes of its species, so you need a big tank to keep more than one. 150 mm.

◀ Red-fin Shark

Like the Red-tailed Black Shark, lives in Thailand, and is equally possessive of its territory. Good at clearing up excess algae on the tank. 150 mm.

Body colour varies

Very flat belly

Barbs

Barbs (pages 16-17) are popular Cyprinids for an aquarium. Barbs need a big tank, good lighting and plenty of oxygen; they must be kept warm, too.

Deep red head ↓

◄ Black Ruby Barb
Popular fish for a community tank. Best kept in groups of six or more because it lives in large shoals in the wild. Comes from Sri Lanka. 65 mm.

Tiger Barb ►
Also called the Sumatra Barb after its home, Sumatra. Illustration shows the commonest variety of this species. May turn nasty and bite other fishes' fins unless it is kept in large shoals. 57 mm.

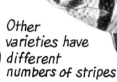

Other varieties have different numbers of stripes

◄ Island Barb
Fond of green foods, e.g. soft lettuce leaves, and eats algae. Shoals usually consist of one male and several females, as males may fight. From Sumatra and Indonesia. 50 mm.

Cherry Barb ►
In the breeding season, the male is a very bright red. Prefers a densely-planted tank. Best kept in twos or threes in community tanks. Comes from Sri Lanka. 50 mm.

Male

Females have yellowish fins

Barbs

Golden Barb ▶
Looks a bit like a small Goldfish. No-one knows which country it originally came from because it is very easy to breed and all specimens are now bred in captivity. 60 mm.

Colour of the fins varies

▲ Tinfoil Barb
Comes from Borneo, Thailand and Indonesia. Often kept by aquarists because of its attractive colouring and quiet nature, but it soon outgrows the tank and may swallow the other fishes as food. 300 mm.

▼ Rosy Barb
An old favourite for community tanks since it is not difficult to keep or to breed. Fairly big and hardy. Comes from India. 100 mm.

Fins are transparent

Rasboras

Rasboras (pages 18-19) are ideal Cyprinids for an aquarium. Most species are easy to breed and feed, and are not aggressive. Rasboras are active swimmers.

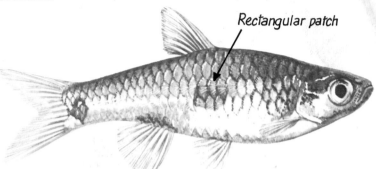

Rectangular patch

▲ Elegant Rasbora
A typical Rasbora, slender in shape and easy to keep. Has no particular preferences regarding food or water. Native homes are Malaysia and Indonesia. 140 mm.

▼ Pearly Rasbora
Also known as the Ceylonese Fire Barb as it is similar in colour to the flowers of the Ceylonese Fire Tree, found in Sri Lanka. Lives in quiet mountain streams in Sri Lanka. 40 mm.

Females have yellowish fins

Male

Dark, cone-shaped mark

◄ Harlequin Fish
One of the most popular fishes for community tanks. Lives wild in Thailand, Indonesia and Sumatra, but is also bred in fish farms in large numbers. 40 mm.

Rasboras

Spotted Rasbora ▶

Sometimes called the
Dwarf Rasbora. Not a fish
for the beginner, because it
must be kept in mature,
acidic water. Best kept in a
separate tank with about a
dozen of its
species. From
SE Asia. 25 mm.

▼ Scissortail Rasbora

Named after the way its
tail fins move, like scissor
blades. An active fish, one
of the most popular
choices for community
tanks. Found
in SE Asia.
110 mm.

Black spots

White Cloud
Mountain Minnow ▶

Lives wild in China, often
in quite cool streams. Easy
to breed, so it is often seen
in community
tanks.
45 mm.

Danios

Danios are lively, shoaling Cyprinids, easy to feed and breed. Most species are small. Danios are ideal for a community tank.

◀ Zebra Danio
An extremely popular fish for community tanks as it is easily bred and looks very striking swimming in shoals. Originally came from paddy fields in India. 50 mm.

Pearl Danio ▶
The original fish had a pearly sheen and lived in rice paddy fields in SE Asia. Now very popular and bred in several colours. 60 mm.

Colouring changes in different lighting conditions

Female

Males are slimmer

◀ Spotted Danio
Originally came from Burma. Like all Danios, prefers to live in a shoal, but a mated pair will stay together all their lives. Another popular fish for community tanks. 40 mm.

Leopard Danio ▶
An interesting result of a variation produced in the Zebra Danio strain. Has random spots instead of regular stripes. The female is fatter than the male. 50 mm.

Male

Livebearing Toothcarps

Livebearing Toothcarps (pages 21-23) come from tropical parts of North, Central and South America. The males fertilize the eggs inside the females using a gonopodium, a modified anal fin. The eggs hatch inside the females and the young fry swim out. Many species of Livebearing Toothcarps (Latin family name: *Poeciliidae*) are hardy and beautiful.

Sailfin Molly ▶

There are two species of Sailfin Molly, but they are very difficult to tell apart. Only the male has the "sailfin".
Male 110 mm.
Female 130 mm.

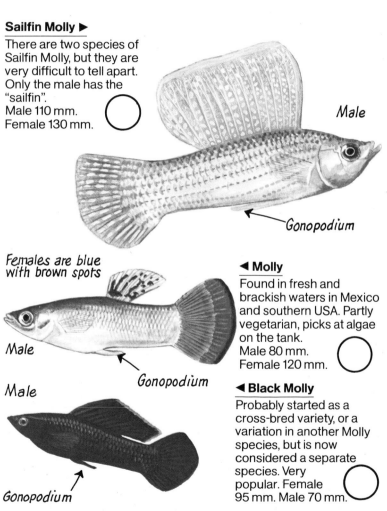

Male

Gonopodium

Females are blue with brown spots

Male

Gonopodium

Male

Gonopodium

◀ Molly

Found in fresh and brackish waters in Mexico and southern USA. Partly vegetarian, picks at algae on the tank.
Male 80 mm.
Female 120 mm.

◀ Black Molly

Probably started as a cross-bred variety, or a variation in another Molly species, but is now considered a separate species. Very popular. Female 95 mm. Male 70 mm.

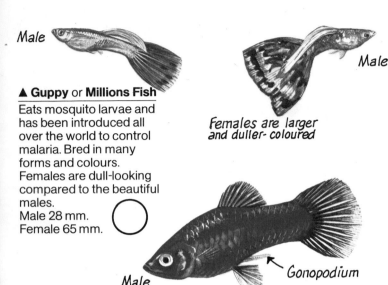

Male

Male

▲ Guppy or Millions Fish
Eats mosquito larvae and has been introduced all over the world to control malaria. Bred in many forms and colours. Females are dull-looking compared to the beautiful males.
Male 28 mm.
Female 65 mm.

Females are larger and duller-coloured

Male

Gonopodium

▲ Platy
Like the Guppy, popular because it is undemanding and easy to breed. Wild form, from Central America, is rare. Many new varieties have been bred. Male 50 mm. Female 65 mm.

▼ Swordtail
Popular fish, famous for the male's long tail fin. Original fish (from Central America) was green. Now bred in other colours as well.
Female 110 mm.
Male 100 mm.

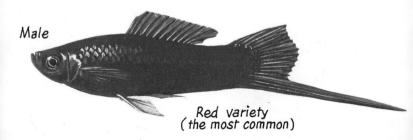

Male

Red variety (the most common)

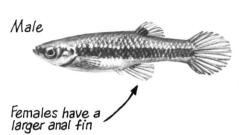

Male

Females have a
larger anal fin

◀ Mosquito Fish

One of the smallest
vertebrates in the world.
In stagnant pools may be
mistaken for a mosquito
larva. From southern USA.
Must not be kept with
large fishes.
Female 35 mm.
Male 20 mm.

▼ Pike Top Minnow

An aggressive fish shaped
like a miniature Pike.
Comes from Central and
South America. Should be
kept alone, or with
a mate.
Male 100 mm.
Female 150 mm.

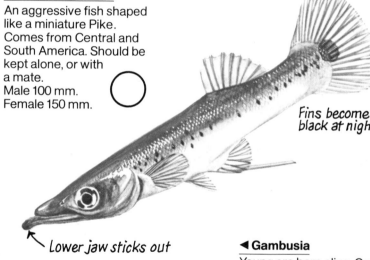

Fins become
black at night

Lower jaw sticks out

Male

◀ Gambusia

Young are born alive. Can
live in quite cool water,
preferably with a little salt.
Best kept in a small shoal
made up mainly of
females, in a big tank.
Comes from Texas,
USA.
Male 35 mm.
Female 65 mm.

Killifishes

Killifishes (pages 24-27) live in seasonal pools in various parts of the world, including India and the USA. Some species die after one year but their eggs survive by drying up until the next rains come. Killifishes (Latin family name: *Cyprinodontidae*) are often brightly-coloured.

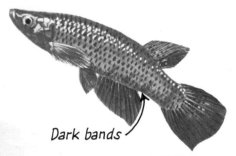

Dark bands

◄ Firemouth Epiplatys

Other names include the Red-chinned Panchax. Originally came from Ghana, but there are many aquarium-bred varieties. Breeders transport the dried eggs in boiled peat. 65 mm.

▼ Striped or Sparkling Panchax

Most Panchax fishes have a light-sensitive spot on the head. Spot is so well-developed in this species that it is almost a primitive eye. From India. 100 mm.

▲ Playfair's Panchax

Unusual because its scales stick out slightly, especially on its back. Comes from fresh and brackish waters in East Africa. 100 mm.

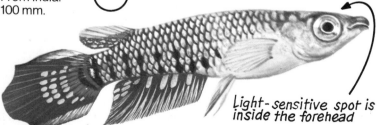

Light-sensitive spot is inside the forehead

Females are less vivid

Male

Male

Females are greenish with brown spots

◀ Day's Killifish
Also called The Killifish and the Ceylon Panchax (after its home, Sri Lanka). Pounces on food falling on the water surface, like a Pike. 70 mm.

◀ Spanish Killi
Generally peaceful, but active. Becoming rare, as it has to compete with other species introduced into southern Spain, where it lives, to control malaria (spread by by mosquitoes). 50 mm.

American Flagfish ▶
Plant-eater from Florida, USA. Rather shy. Stripes look a little like the Stars and Stripes (flag of the USA). Colouring varies. 70 mm.

Argentine Pearl Fish ▶
Found in seasonal pools and lakes in Argentina. Sturdier than most of the Killifish species, and can be kept in community tanks. 70 mm.

Shining spots

Females are brownish-yellow

Male

25

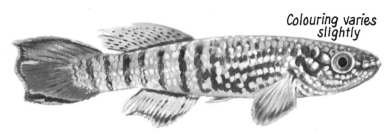

Colouring varies slightly

▼ Plumed Lyretail

West Nigerian fish famous for the male's fins, which look like the feathers of the Lyrebird (a tropical bird from Australia). 60 mm.

▲ Blue Gularis

Lives in seasonal pools in Nigeria and Cameroon. It is born, mates and dies in one year. 100 mm.

Male

Male

Guenther's Nothobranch ▶

Typical East African Killifish. Too aggressive to be kept in community tanks, so is usually only kept by specialists. 70 mm.

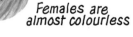

Females are almost colourless

◀ Japanese Medaka

Ideal for beginners as it can be kept in tropical or cold water tanks. Red variety is the most common, but original form, found in Japan, is grey-green. 45 mm.

Red variety

▲ Golden Ear

Found in fresh and slightly salty waters in southern USA. Can live in outdoor ponds when the temperature is over over 15° Centigrade. 80 mm.

▼ Cuban Rivulus

Also called the Green or Brown Rivulus. Like all Rivulus fishes, is peaceful and not at all fussy. Lives at the surface. Best kept in small groups. 50 mm.

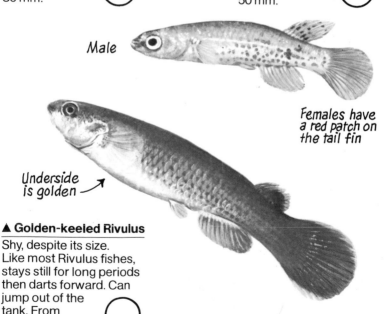

Male

Females have a red patch on the tail fin

Underside is golden →

▲ Golden-keeled Rivulus

Shy, despite its size. Like most Rivulus fishes, stays still for long periods then darts forward. Can jump out of the tank. From Guyana. 95 mm.

Cichlids

Cichlids (pages 28-33) are Perch-like fishes from Africa, Central and South America. A few species live in Asia. Cichlids (Latin family name *Cichlidae*) tend to be agressive and defensive of their territory. Many of the African Cichlids are "characters", and are very intelligent.

Red on throat and belly

▲ Firemouth Cichlid

Name comes from its red underside. Colouring is particularly strong at breeding time. From the USA. Wild specimens 150 mm. Usually much smaller in captivity.

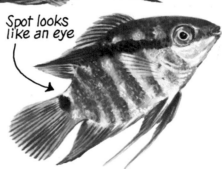

Spot looks like an eye

▼ Convict Cichlid

Another Cichlid from North America. Not often seen in community tanks because it is aggressive. Name comes from the stripes. 150 mm.

▲ Festive Cichlid

Often kept in community tanks because it is peaceful and often does not reach full size in an aquarium. From the Central Amazon. 150 mm.

▼ Jewel Cichlid

Widespread in tropical Africa. Very intelligent, often studied by scientists. Must be kept alone in a big tank as it is very aggressive, but makes a good parent. 150 mm.

Body flecked with glistening spots

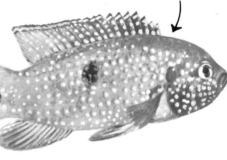

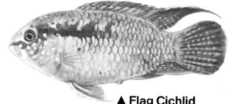

▲ Flag Cichlid

Another peaceful Cichlid often kept in community tanks. Unlike many large Cichlids, does not uproot plants. Comes from the Amazon region. 80 mm.

▼ Keyhole Cichlid

Large fish from Guiana. Most specimens are bred in captivity now. Well-behaved, except at spawning time. Popular for community tanks. 100 mm.

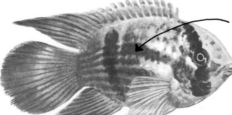

"Keyhole" marking changes with moods

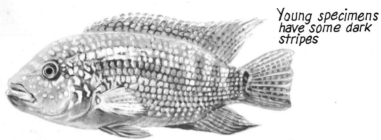

Young specimens have some dark stripes

▲ Jack Dempsey

Very aggressive fish, named after the famous boxer. Can only be kept with large, tough fishes. Tears up plants. Comes from the Amazon. 200 mm.

▼ Blue Acara

Popular choice for large tanks, although it is likely to dig up all the plants. Found in Venezuela, Trinidad and Panama. 180 mm.

▼ Oscar

Big fish found in all types of water in South America. Very intelligent and often kept, but is aggressive, too, and may bite. 300 mm.

Background colour varies

Females are greenish-yellow

Male

◀ Golden-eyed Dwarf Cichlid

Good Cichlid for a community tank. A pair may breed if there is a shelter (e.g. a flower pot) to lay the eggs in. From Guiana.
Female 60 mm.
Male 70 mm.

Yellow Dwarf Cichlid ▶

The female lays eggs on the "roof" of an under-water cave. Only happy in soft, mildly acidic water. Comes from Paraguay.
Female 45 mm.
Male 50 mm.

Male

Females are lemon yellow

◀ Borelli's Dwarf Cichlid

Lives in shaded waters in Argentina. Prefers to swim near the bottom of the tank. Has a rather bull-nosed profile.
Male 70 mm.
Female 60 mm.

◀ Ram

Sometimes called the Dwarf Butterfly Cichlid because of its lovely colouring. Very popular. Originally came from Venezuela but most are bred in captivity.
Female 65 mm.
Male 70 mm.

Wild
variety

Veiltail
(Exotic
variety)

▲ Angelfish

Probably the best-known
tropical fish. Original wild
form lived in the Amazon.
Now bred in many exotic
varieties in fish farms
all over
the world.
110 mm.

▼ Discus

Considered the king of
tropical fishes because of
its regal bearing. Feeds
the fry on mucus from its
body. Needs soft, acidic
water. From
the Amazon.
150 mm.

Stripes are good
camouflage

◄ Dwarf Egyptian
Mouthbrooder

So-called because the fry
hide in the female's mouth.
Quiet and easy to breed.
One of the many Cichlids
from East Africa.
Male 75 mm.
Female 70 mm.

Eye spot

▲ Eye-spot Cichlid

Famous for the imitation
eye marking on its tail.
An aggressive predator
from S. America, where
it is caught as food and by
anglers.
Hard to keep.
450 mm.

▼ Zebra Nyasa Cichlid

Also known as the Blue
Cichlid. Comes from Lake
Malawi (formerly Lake
Nyasa), in Africa. Prefers
hard, alkaline water. Males
and females
look the same.
150 mm.

Female

Kribensis ▶

Becomes very bright when
paired with a mate. Comes
from Cameroon. Most
specimens are bed in
captivity. Very
popular.
Female 75 mm.
Male 100 mm.

◀ Nyasa Golden Cichlid

Another Cichlid from Lake
Malawi, Africa. Mature
males are black. Females
and young males are
golden. Aggressive.
Keep only with
large fishes.
130 mm.

Labyrinth Fishes

Labyrinth Fishes (pages 34-36) are named after a compartment in their heads. Labyrinth Fishes (Latin family name: *Anabantidae*) can come to the surface, gulp in air and force it into the labyrinth where oxygen is extracted and passed into the bloodstream.

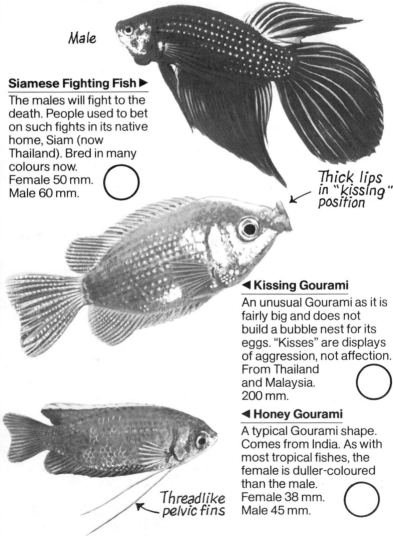

Male

Siamese Fighting Fish ▶
The males will fight to the death. People used to bet on such fights in its native home, Siam (now Thailand). Bred in many colours now.
Female 50 mm.
Male 60 mm.

Thick lips in "kissing" position

◀ Kissing Gourami
An unusual Gourami as it is fairly big and does not build a bubble nest for its eggs. "Kisses" are displays of aggression, not affection.
From Thailand and Malaysia.
200 mm.

◀ Honey Gourami
A typical Gourami shape. Comes from India. As with most tropical fishes, the female is duller-coloured than the male.
Female 38 mm.
Male 45 mm.

Threadlike pelvic fins

Most Labyrinth Fishes keep their eggs in a "bubble nest." The male builds the nest by gulping in air and spitting out lots of tiny, saliva-coated bubbles. These float on the surface in a mass.

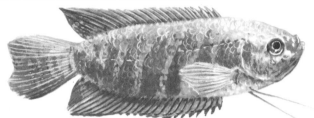

▲ Giant Gourami

Very easy to breed. Lays as many as a thousand eggs in its bubble nest. Shy. Can grow very big in a really large aquarium.
Male 100 mm.
Female 90 mm.

▲ Dwarf Gourami

The best-known Gourami. Shy, but easy to keep.
Male 60 mm.
Female 50 mm.

◄ Three-spot Gourami

Only has two real spots (the third is the eye). Easy to breed. Many new varieties have been bred from the original wild form.
110 mm.

Colouring varies

Chocolate Gourami ►

Hides its young in its mouth. Rarely kept, as it eats only live food and is hard to breed.
Male 60 mm.
Female 50 mm.

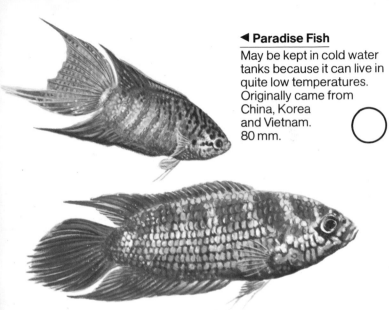

◀ Paradise Fish

May be kept in cold water tanks because it can live in quite low temperatures. Originally came from China, Korea and Vietnam. 80 mm.

▲ Comb-tailed Paradise Fish

Can be vicious. After a few years, develops a dark patch behind the dorsal fin. Can be bred in captivity. Comes from Sri Lanka. 150 mm.

▼ Climbing Perch

Can not only breathe air at the surface, but will climb out of the water to do so, and its tank must have a lid. Widespread from India to the Philippines. 200 mm.

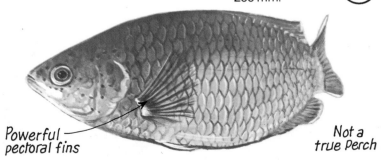

Powerful pectoral fins

Not a true Perch

Catfishes

Many species of Catfishes (pages 37-39) are found all over the world. Catfishes (Latin family name: *Siluroidea*) are generally hardy, and are usually active at night. Most species live near the bottom and search for food with their barbels.

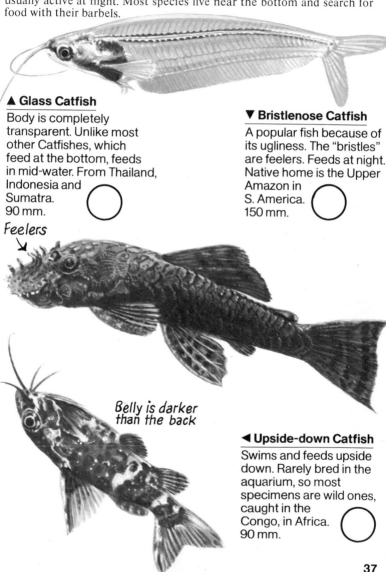

▲ Glass Catfish

Body is completely transparent. Unlike most other Catfishes, which feed at the bottom, feeds in mid-water. From Thailand, Indonesia and Sumatra. 90 mm.

▼ Bristlenose Catfish

A popular fish because of its ugliness. The "bristles" are feelers. Feeds at night. Native home is the Upper Amazon in S. America. 150 mm.

Feelers

Belly is darker than the back

◄ Upside-down Catfish

Swims and feeds upside down. Rarely bred in the aquarium, so most specimens are wild ones, caught in the Congo, in Africa. 90 mm.

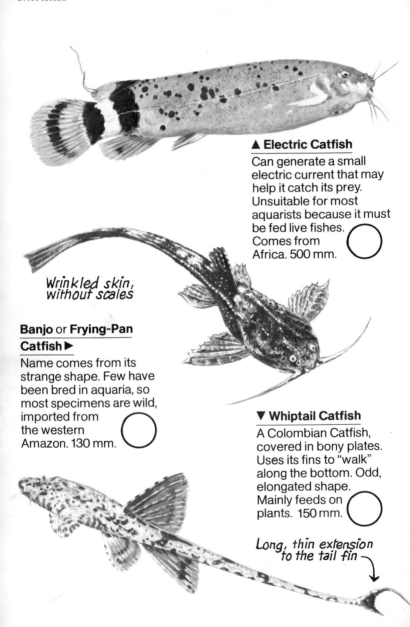

▲ Electric Catfish

Can generate a small electric current that may help it catch its prey. Unsuitable for most aquarists because it must be fed live fishes. Comes from Africa. 500 mm.

Wrinkled skin, without scales

Banjo or Frying-Pan Catfish ▶

Name comes from its strange shape. Few have been bred in aquaria, so most specimens are wild, imported from the western Amazon. 130 mm.

▼ Whiptail Catfish

A Colombian Catfish, covered in bony plates. Uses its fins to "walk" along the bottom. Odd, elongated shape. Mainly feeds on plants. 150 mm.

Long, thin extension to the tail fin

Corydoras Catfishes

Catfishes of the Corydoras genus (on this page only) are very popular. These fishes are peaceful, bottom-living scavengers. Corydoras Catfishes are covered in bony, overlapping plates, not scales. They all have barbels.

Barbel

◄ Bronze Corydoras

One of the most popular Corydoras Catfishes, bred in large numbers for the aquarium. Originally came from Brazil and other countries in S. America. 75 mm.

Leopard Corydoras ►

An Amazonian Catfish, very well suited to community tanks. A good scavenger; will clean up leftover food on the bottom. 65 mm.

◄ Albino Catfish

An albino Corydoras bred from the Brazilian Peppered Corydoras (now quite rare), a species that sometimes produces albino forms. Male 70 mm. Female 75 mm.

Black Spotted

Corydoras ►

Widespread in northern parts of S. America. All specimens are caught in the wild. There are no records of its being bred in captivity. 65 mm.

Dark stripe through the eye

Loaches

Loaches (on this page only) have long, eel-like bodies. They live on the bottom – some even bury themselves – and search out food with the barbels around their small mouths. Loaches (Latin family name: *Cobitidae*) come from Europe and Asia.

▲ Coolie Loach
A worm-like fish from Indonesia, Sumatra and Java. Spends most of its time hiding behind rocks or plants.
Easy to keep.
110 mm.

▼ Clown Loach
Its distinctive, clown-like colouring makes it a favourite with aquarists. Found in Thailand and neighbouring countries. Swims jerkily.
200 mm.

▼ Banded Loach
One of several *Botia* fishes that are the same shape, but have different colour patterns. All are from the Far East.
Easy to keep.
200 mm.

Colour of the stripes varies

Pencilfishes, Butterfly Fish

The fishes on this page and the following pages belong to fairly small families of fishes. Sometimes only one species is shown to represent the family, sometimes two or more are illustrated.

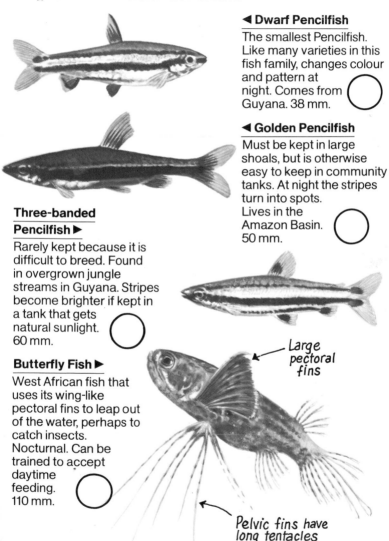

◄ Dwarf Pencilfish

The smallest Pencilfish. Like many varieties in this fish family, changes colour and pattern at night. Comes from Guyana. 38 mm.

◄ Golden Pencilfish

Must be kept in large shoals, but is otherwise easy to keep in community tanks. At night the stripes turn into spots. Lives in the Amazon Basin. 50 mm.

Three-banded Pencilfish ►

Rarely kept because it is difficult to breed. Found in overgrown jungle streams in Guyana. Stripes become brighter if kept in a tank that gets natural sunlight. 60 mm.

Butterfly Fish ►

West African fish that uses its wing-like pectoral fins to leap out of the water, perhaps to catch insects. Nocturnal. Can be trained to accept daytime feeding. 110 mm.

Large pectoral fins

Pelvic fins have long tentacles

Pufferfishes, Bumblebee Fish

Common Pufferfish ▶
Like all Pufferfishes, can blow itself up like a balloon if alarmed. Attacks other fishes' fins, so rarely kept in home aquaria.
From India.
150 mm.

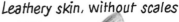
Leathery skin, without scales

Markings look like figures-of-eight

▲ Figure-eight Pufferfish
Less aggressive than the Common Pufferfish. May be kept in community tanks. Needs plenty of space to stake out its territory. Comes from SE Asia.
150 mm.

▼ Green Pufferfish
Found on the shores of the Indian Ocean. Can live in fresh, brackish or salt water. The least aggressive Pufferfish.
180 mm.

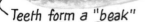
Teeth form a "beak"

◀ Bumblebee Fish
One of several species of Gobies, all very alike. Best kept on its own in brackish water. Clings to the tank glass with a sucker. Comes from Indonesia.
50 mm.

Pelvic fins form a sucker

Leaf Fish, Badis, Halfbeak, Foureyes

Hangs
motionless,
usually
head down

◀ Leaf Fish

South American fish
camouflaged as a dead
leaf. Eats small fishes
fooled by its disguise. Can
be kept in community
tanks where there
are no small
fishes. 75 mm.

▼ Badis

Belongs to the greedy and
aggressive Nandidae fish
family, but is unusually
well-behaved. Males are
possessive of
their territory.
From SE Asia.
65 mm.

▼ Halfbeak

Member of the
Dermogenys fish family
found in Thailand, Malaysia
and Singapore. All are live-
bearers. Males
may fight.
Male 65 mm.
Female 90 mm.

Male

Females are brownish
and have rounded bellies

▼ Foureyes

Eyes are divided; can see
above and below the
surface at once. Eats
floating food (flakes are
ideal). Needs an "island"
so it can rest partly out of
the water. From
northern South
America. 250 mm.

Long lower jaw

Rainbowfishes, Glassfishes

Celebes Rainbowfish ▶

Famous for its shimmering colours. Rarely kept because it is timid and must live in mildly salty water. From lakes in Sulawesi. 70 mm.

Females have shorter dorsal and anal fins

Male

▲ Australian Rainbowfish

Also called the Dwarf Rainbowfish. Happy in small groups in home aquaria. Lives in shoals in warm waters near coasts of northeastern Australia. 90 mm.

Fins are divided

▼ Indian Glassfish

Delicate, almost transparent fish found in Burma, India and Pakistan. Often seen in home aquaria, although it needs slightly brackish water. 75 mm.

◄ Siamese Glassfish

Less colourful but more aggressive than the Indian Glassfish, so less often kept by aquarists. Comes from Thailand. 75 mm.

Sunfishes, Hatchetfishes

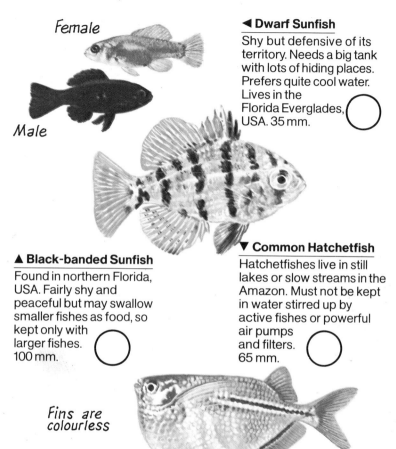

Female

Male

◀ Dwarf Sunfish

Shy but defensive of its territory. Needs a big tank with lots of hiding places. Prefers quite cool water. Lives in the Florida Everglades, USA. 35 mm.

▲ Black-banded Sunfish

Found in northern Florida, USA. Fairly shy and peaceful but may swallow smaller fishes as food, so kept only with larger fishes. 100 mm.

▼ Common Hatchetfish

Hatchetfishes live in still lakes or slow streams in the Amazon. Must not be kept in water stirred up by active fishes or powerful air pumps and filters. 65 mm.

Fins are colourless

Marbled Hatchetfish ▶

The prettiest of the Hatchetfishes. May hide much of the time as it is rather shy. From the Amazon region. 65 mm.

Headstander, Anostomus, etc.

Spotted Headstander ▶

Even the shoals of fry swim with their heads down. Makes a loud "clicking" noise. Shy, but suitable for community tanks.
From Guiana.
75 mm.

Most scales have a dark spot

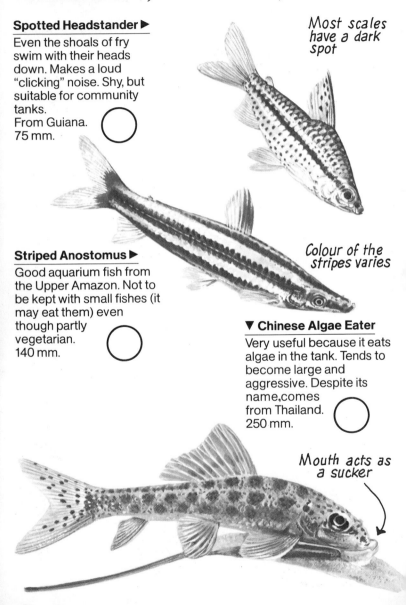

Striped Anostomus ▶

Good aquarium fish from the Upper Amazon. Not to be kept with small fishes (it may eat them) even though partly vegetarian.
140 mm.

Colour of the stripes varies

▼ Chinese Algae Eater

Very useful because it eats algae in the tank. Tends to become large and aggressive. Despite its name, comes from Thailand.
250 mm.

Mouth acts as a sucker

Knifefish, Archerfish, Elephant Fish

Arched back

Very flat body

▲ Clown Knifefish
Quickly outgrows most tanks and swallows other fishes. Caught as food in Thailand, India and Burma.
Active mainly at night.
710 mm.

▼ Archerfish
Can "shoot down" insects with a jet of water from its mouth. Widespread in brackish waters in Asia. Never bred in captivity.
200 mm.

▼ Long-nosed Elephant Fish
Belongs to the Mormyridae fish family found in Africa. Has poor eyesight and relies on its lateral line. Hard to keep. Needs a tank with a deep, muddy bottom.
250 mm.

Burrows with its long snout

Goldfishes

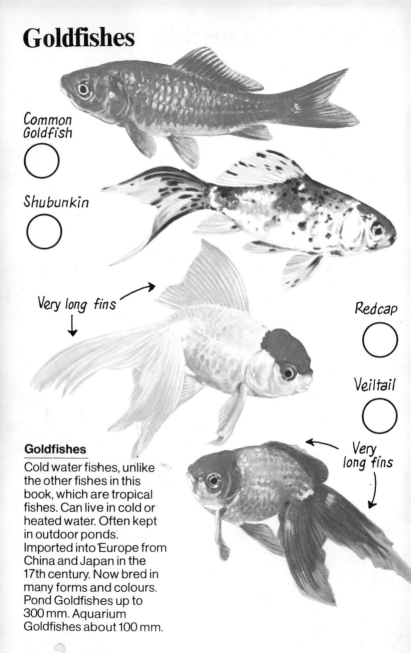

Common
Goldfish
◯

Shubunkin
◯

Very long fins

Redcap
◯

Veiltail
◯

Very
long fins

Goldfishes

Cold water fishes, unlike
the other fishes in this
book, which are tropical
fishes. Can live in cold or
heated water. Often kept
in outdoor ponds.
Imported into Europe from
China and Japan in the
17th century. Now bred in
many forms and colours.
Pond Goldfishes up to
300 mm. Aquarium
Goldfishes about 100 mm.

Setting up an aquarium

If you want to keep aquarium fishes, follow the directions on the next few pages carefully. They show you how to set up a tank with a heater, air pump, filter, lights and plants.

Goldfishes prefer a temperature of 16°C, so if you are going to keep only Goldfishes, you do not need a heater. All the other fishes in this book need a temperature of about 24°C, so you must heat the water.

Buy the best equipment you can afford. The staff in most aquarists' shops and petshops will be able to advise you. Read the instructions on each piece of equipment, and always ask a responsible adult to check electrical equipment for you before you plug it in.

The tank

Buy a good, modern, all-glass tank, the kind that is glued together with a silicone sealer. Secondhand tanks are often advertised quite cheaply in local newspapers.

Buy as large a tank as you can. Fishes need lots of space. It is easier to maintain a large volume of water than a small one, too.

To keep a dozen small community fishes, or five Goldfishes about nine centimetres long, you need a tank that holds at least 75 litres of water. This means the tank must be at least 65 centimetres long, 35 centimetres wide and 37 centimetres high.

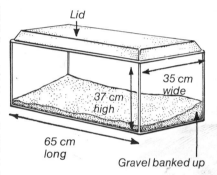

Lid

35 cm wide

37 cm high

65 cm long

Gravel banked up

Preparation

Scrub the tank thoroughly inside and out. Don't use soap or detergents because these are harmful to fishes. Polish the glass with a soft, clean cloth.

The tank bottom should be lined with a bucketful of gravel from a petshop. Wash the gravel well. (A good way to do this is to push a hosepipe to the bottom of a bucket half full of gravel.)

Bank the gravel in the tank so that it slopes down towards the front. Dirt will then roll to the front where it can easily be siphoned out.

Position the tank before you fill it. Never move a full tank because the slopping of the water may twist the tank and crack the glass. Place the tank on a solid, flat table in a light place (but away from direct sunlight as this encourages algae to grow).

Water

Ordinary tap water is best for an aquarium, because it is clean and sterile. However, tap water contains chlorine, which can harm the fishes. Let the water stand overnight in a bucket. By morning, the chlorine will have disappeared naturally. (You can remove chlorine from tap water by boiling the water if you need it in a hurry. Stir the water briskly afterwards to replace the oxygen driven off during boiling.)

To avoid disturbing the gravel in the tank, rest a saucer on the tank bottom and pour water slowly onto the saucer. Stop when the tank is about two-thirds full.

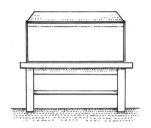

▲ Place your tank on a strong stand or similar support. Never move it when it's full.

Heating the water

A combined heater and thermostat

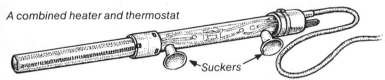

◄Suckers

Heater

The simplest kind of heater is a combined thermostat and heater. This should be fixed to the inside of the tank glass, near the bottom, using plastic suckers.

Never switch on the heater when it is out of water, as it could overheat and crack the glass or damage the element.

Wattage

For a tank measuring 65 x 35 x 37 centimetres you need one 100 watt heater, or two 60 watt heaters placed level with each other. (Watts are units of electric power.)

If your tank is in a cool room, or in a room that gets cold at night, increase the wattage by about one half, i.e. use one 150 watt heater or two 75 watt heaters. If the tank is kept outside in an unheated shed, double the wattage.

Thermometer

You must have a good, accurate thermometer to check water temperature.

Choose one that can be fixed with suckers to the glass, underwater, or a plastic strip thermometer. This is the most reliable kind. The plastic strip thermometer contains crystals that glow and light up a number, showing the exact temperature. The strip is stuck to the outside of the tank glass.

Thermometers should be placed half-way up the tank wall at the opposite end to the heater.

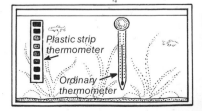

Plastic strip thermometer

Ordinary thermometer

Fitting an air pump

Air pumps add oxygen to the water. They can also run a filter to clean the water. Air pumps are useful, but not essential. Before you buy one, ask to hear it running. The cheaper models are very noisy.

An air pump consists of a pump that forces air down an airline into the water. The air is usually diffused through a small air stone at the end of the airline.

Air pumps should be mounted above the level of the water in the tank, to stop water running back down the airline. Fix the end of the airline to the glass inside the tank using plastic suckers.

If your tank is in a room where there is cigarette smoke, it is a good idea to put the pump in another room. Run the airline through a small hole drilled in the wall.

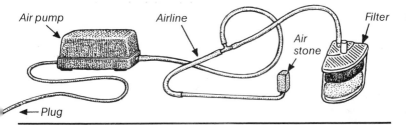

Air pump · Airline · Filter · Air stone · Plug

Fitting a filter

Filters clean the water and keep it moving. A cheap, simple kind of filter is the corner or box filter (triangular or rectangular shape). This sort of filter is a container packed with absorbent synthetic wool that traps waste matter in the water. An airline from the air pump goes into the container and keeps water flowing through it.

Use nylon or terylene wool in the filter, not cotton wool (this rots). When the wool gets dirty, replace it. A handful of charcoal in a small bag (e.g. cut out of an old pair of tights) will chemically purify the water. Weigh down the filter with a rock or some gravel in the bottom, then add the wool, and place the bag of charcoal on top. Position the filter in a corner of the tank, connected up to the airline.

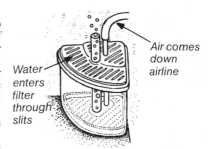

Air comes down airline · Water enters filter through slits

▲ Corner filter (before packing)

Wool · Charcoal · Gravel

▲ Corner filter (after packing)

Lighting

To make the lighting look natural, and to avoid algae growing across the side of the tank, place the tank away from windows and light it from above.

Ordinary bulbs are cheap to buy, but expensive to run, and they heat the water (this is very bad for cold water fishes). Fluorescent strip lights may seem expensive but are worth buying because they last a long time, and do not heat the water.

For a tank measuring 65 x 35 x 37 centimetres, you need either two 40 watt ordinary bulbs, or one 20 watt fluorescent strip light about 60 centimetres long.

If your tank has a lid, set the lights into this. If you are covering the tank with a sheet of glass standing on small blocks, or have no lid at all, simply position the lights above the tank.

Wire ordinary bulbs in a row inside the lid. Protect the fittings from condensation by covering them with a bit of bicycle inner tubing. Mount strip lights inside the lid and protect the ends with a smear of silicone sealer. Each strip light will have a starter. Hang this on the wall behind the tank.

Avoid sudden changes in lighting because these will frighten the fishes. If the room and the tank are dark, switch on the room lights before you switch on the lights in the tank. An aquarium should generally have eight to ten hours of light a day.

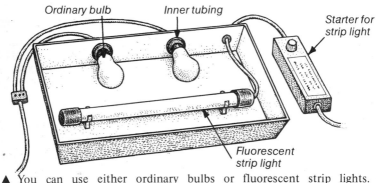

Ordinary bulb   Inner tubing   Starter for strip light

Fluorescent strip light

▲ You can use either ordinary bulbs or fluorescent strip lights.

Decorations

Artificial decorations, such as plastic sunken ships and mermaids, usually look a bit odd, and they trap dirt. Good alternatives are a large piece of bogwood (from a petshop) or one or two rocks. Hard rock, like granite, is best. Seashells and soft rocks dissolve minerals into the water that are harmful to freshwater fishes.

If looking after lots of plants seems too difficult, buy plastic ones. Some of these are very attractive and convincing.

Plants

Plants add oxygen to the water, they provide shade and shelter for the fishes, and they make the tank look attractive. However, all plants need a lot of attention.

For a 65 centimetre tank you should have about 100 plants (if you have fewer than this, you may get problems with algae). This can be expensive, so buy plants that grow quickly, such as *Elodea,* or plants that have "daughters", such as *Vallisneria.*

Always buy plants from a pet-shop or an aquarists' shop. Garden plants will not do. Read around the subject before you buy, and choose plants that suit the water conditions in your tank.

Rooting

You can simply push the plant roots into the gravel and anchor them with small lead weights or pebbles if necessary. It is better, however, to give plants a good rooting medium, such as moss peat. Soak the peat in rainwater to drain out excess acids and make it water-logged. After a few weeks, take it out, squeeze it, and spread it over the tank bottom in a layer about three centimetres deep. Cover the peat with a layer of pinhead size gravel about two centimetres deep. Bank up the gravel at the back.

Arrangement

Arrange big plants around the back or sides of the tank, and smaller ones at the front. You can root two or three plants of the same species together, in clumps. Avoid symmetrical arrangements, because these look rather dull.

Plant care

Occasionally add a little aquatic plant food to the water. Every week, check all the plants and remove dead or dying leaves. If the plants are turning yellow, try increasing the hours of light.

Let the plants settle in for a week before you add the fishes. In this time you can check that the air pump, filter, lights, heater and thermostat are working properly.

▼ All these water plants are fairly hardy and easy to look after.

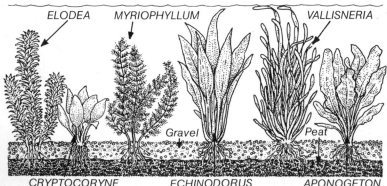

ELODEA   MYRIOPHYLLUM   VALLISNERIA

Gravel   Peat

CRYPTOCORYNE   ECHINODORUS   APONOGETON

Stocking the aquarium

Choosing your fishes
Start with a community tank made up of a dozen or so fishes that are easy to keep. A good mixture might consist of Guppies, Mollies, Angelfishes, Platies, Neon Tetras and a Corydoras Catfish. Buy two or three fishes to begin with and build up slowly.

Buy fishes from reputable dealers and never buy "cheap" ones. The fishes should look colourful, clean and lively. Don't buy baby fishes, as they may die. Young fishes are about half the adult size quoted in books. Check the fishes for signs of disease, especially White Spot and Fungus (see page 56).

Taking your fishes home
The fishes will probably be given to you in a sealed bag half full of water. Pack the bag in a warm, dark, insulated container, such as a polystyrene box or a carrier bag filled with woollens.

When you get home, open the bag very gently, using scissors. Float it upright in the tank. Don't turn on the tank lights yet.

After about 20 minutes, the temperature of the water in the bag should be the same as the temperature of the tank water. Let the fishes swim out of the bag, or tip the bag gently to make them swim out.

Leave the tank lights off for a day or so, to let the fishes settle in quietly. Don't feed the fishes for at least a day.

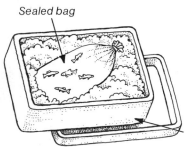

Sealed bag

Polystyrene box

▼ When you get home, open the top of the fishes' bag and float the bag upright in the tank.

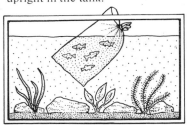

▼ Once the water in the bag is the same temperature as the tank water, you can let the fishes swim out.

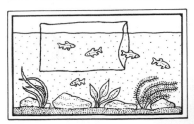

Maintenance

Daily jobs
Feeding time is the best time to do these jobs.

● Look at the tank and tidy it up. Remove dead or dying leaves, pick up fallen ornaments, etc.

● Check the fishes for signs of disease.

● Make sure that the water is at the correct temperature, and that all the equipment is working properly.

Weekly jobs
The most important task of all is the weekly partial water change.

The day before you change the water, fill a bucket with tap water and let it stand. The next day, siphon out 20 per cent of the water in the tank (see pictures 1 and 2 below), i.e. 15 litres from a 75 litre tank. Boil some tap water and add enough to the bucket of prepared water to bring its temperature up to that of the water in the tank. Pour the bucket of water very slowly into the tank.

If you don't change some of the water in the tank once a week, the tank will get so filthy that you will have to empty out all the water and the fishes and scrub the tank clean. Drastic changes of any kind make fishes weak, so it is dangerous to take them out of mature, dirty water and put them in raw, very clean tap water.

Monthly jobs
● Check the air pump, lights, heater, thermostat, filter and all airlines and wiring.

● Change the wool in the filter.

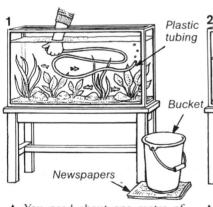

Plastic tubing

Bucket

Newspapers

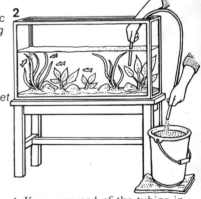

▲ You need about one metre of plastic tubing for siphoning. Put it in the tank and let it fill up with water. Meanwhile, get a bucket and place it next to the tank. Put it on some newspapers, in case you spill any water.

▲ Keep one end of the tubing in the tank and hold the other end over the bucket. Siphon out about 20 per cent of the water in the tank. While you are doing this, you can "hoover" the gravel with the end of the tubing in the tank. Dirt and waste are sucked out of the tank.

Problems with algae

Algae are simple plants, usually green, but sometimes blue or brown. Algae can cloud the water or form slimy carpets of weed inside the tank. They do not harm the fishes, but they can make the tank look dirty.

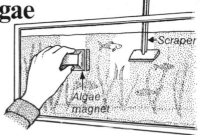

Possible causes of excess algae:
● Too much light. Plants need up to ten hours of light a day. If you have only a few plants, or just plastic ones, cut down the hours of light or reduce the wattage.
● Overfeeding. Fishes will eat whatever you give them. They simply excrete into the water whatever they don't need. Don't overfeed your fishes, as algae flourish in water fouled by waste.
● Dirty water. This encourages

▲ Algae magnets or scrapers will remove algae from an aquarium.

algae, so change some of the tank water at least once a week.

You can scrape algae off the tank from the inside with a scraper (a blade on a handle), or disperse it from the outside with an algae magnet. Some fishes will eat algae, and Catfishes help because they clear up uneaten scraps and keep the tank clean. Snails will not help.

Fish diseases

White Spot and Fungus are common fish diseases. Both are caused by parasites and can be cured by remedies sold at petshops and aquarists' shops. Always check to see whether the disease has been caused by stress as well.

White Spot affects mostly tropical fishes. It causes tiny white spots on the fish's body.

Fungus affects tropical and cold water fishes. It looks like cotton wool growing on the body.

Ask a vet for advice on other, more serious ailments. Fin rot, boils and infected cuts are treated with antibiotics. If your fishes are very ill, you will have to kill them or ask an adult to kill them for you by cutting off their heads. Never flush sick fishes down the toilet. This trans-

fers disease into the country's water system. Throw dead fishes into the dustbin.

Fishes become weak and easily fall ill when they are under stress.
● Don't suddenly change the lighting, water temperature or water quality in your fishes' tank.
● Soap harms fishes. If you have to put your hands in the tank, wash them afterwards, not before.
● Don't handle fishes. Pick them up very gently, with a net.
● Never overcrowd the tank.
● If you notice one fish bullying others, put it in a separate tank.
● Remove any rocks or ornaments that have sharp edges.
● Don't tap on the tank glass. Loud noises send shock waves through the water in the tank.

Feeding

A top quality commercial fish food will give your fishes a balanced diet, but you can add to this with occasional live food or scraps.

Commercial fish foods

These come in various forms: flakes, granules, frozen and freeze-dried. Flakes are the best kind to buy.

Put flakes flat on the water surface for surface feeders; let them drop in sideways for middle and bottom feeders, and crumble flakes up for small fishes.

Live foods

Give your fishes an occasional treat of a live earthworm, slug or greenfly. You can buy specially cultured live fish food such as fruit flies and white worms. Other types of live food, such as water fleas and tubifex worms, can be risky, as they often carry parasites.

Scraps

Plant-eating fishes will eat boiled peas. Squash the peas up for smaller fishes to eat. Grated frozen meat, such as beef heart and chicken livers, is usually popular with meat-eating fishes.

How to feed fishes

The basic rule is: don't overfeed. One flake is a good meal for an average-sized aquarium fish. In general, you should feed a tropical fish, about two centimetres long, one flake one centimetre long twice a day.

It is quite good to make your fishes go without food for a day once in a while, as they would in the wild. For example, you could feed your fishes twice a day for six days and not feed them on the seventh day.

Feed your fishes at a particular part of the tank. All the greedy ones will rush across, making it easy to feed the shy ones separately. This also makes it easier to clear up leftover food.

▲ Give your fishes the correct amount of food twice a day.

When you go away

It is quite safe to leave your fishes without food for a week (even for two weeks if they are adult, healthy fishes). Otherwise, measure out the correct amount of food they will need and leave it with a neighbour. Ask them to feed the fishes once or twice a week. Make sure no-one will overfeed the fishes while you are away.

Leave the lights on if you have a lot of plants in the tank. Otherwise switch them off or ask a neighbour to turn them on every day or so.

Leave the heater on.

Books and magazines

All About Tropical Fish. Derek McInery and Geoffrey Gerard (Harrap).
Naturalist's Guide to Fresh Water Aquarium Fish. J. J. Hoedeman (Oak Tree Press).
The Goldfish. George F. Hervey and Jack Hems (Faber).
Tropical Aquarium Fishes Freshwater and Marine. George Cust and Graham Cox (Hamlyn).
Tropical Freshwater Aquaria. George Cust and Peter Bird (Hamlyn).
The Complete Aquarium Encyclopedia of Tropical Freshwater Fish. Dr. J. D. Van Ramshorst (Elsevier/Phaidon).

Good monthly magazines:

Aquarist and Pondkeeper. The Butts, Half Acre, Brentford, Middlesex.
Practical fishkeeping. EMAP National Publications, Bretton Court, Bretton, Peterborough, Cambs.

Note:
Some manufacturers offer free advisory services; for example, the Aquarian Advisory Service run by Dr. Ford at the Animal Studies Centre, Freeby Lane, Waltham-on-the-Wolds, Melton Mowbray, Leicestershire LE14 4RT.

Societies

There are many advantages in joining an aquarium society, apart from making friends with people who share your interest in aquarium fishes. You will find that you can buy or exchange equipment, plants and books with other members; spare fishes are available cheaply or even free, because members breed their own fishes. Society members often get special vouchers from local aquarist shops, too.

There are hundreds of local aquarium societies in Britain. Most of the aquarium societies in the South belong to the **FBAS** (Federation of British Aquarist Societies); most of those in the North belong to the **FNAS** (Federation of Northern Aquatic Societies).

Ask in your local petshop or aquarist shop for the address of your local aquarium society. Look in *Practical fishkeeping* and *Aquarist* magazines for the addresses of the secretaries of the **FBAS**, **FNAS**, etc. (Always remember to enclose a stamped, self-addressed envelope when writing off to federations or societies for information.)

If you decide to specialize in a particular species or family of aquarium fishes, you may be interested in joining a national society, such as the **GSGB** (Goldfish Society of Great Britain) or the **CAGB** (Catfish Association of Great Britain). You can find the addresses of national societies in aquarist shops and magazines.

Local and national aquarium fish societies hold open shows where the members display their fishes. Sometimes the shows are competitions between members of a society, or between two or more societies. Federations hold larger national or international shows.

Glossary

Barbels – sensitive feelers around some fishes' mouths. Fishes use barbels to find food on the bottom.
Brackish (of water) – slightly salty.
Fry – the young of fishes.
Genus – a group of related species.
Hardness (of water) – a measure of the amount of calcium and magnesium salts in water. Hard water contains a lot of these salts, soft water much less.
Livebearer – a fish that gives birth to live young.
Nocturnal – active at night.
pH value – a measure of the acidity or alkalinity of water. (You can change the pH of the water in your aquarium to suit your fishes by buying special kits, if necessary.)
Predator – an animal that kills and eats other animals.
Shoal – a large group of fishes of the same species that swim together.
Spawn – to produce eggs or young.
Species – a group of animals or plants that look alike and share certain characteristics. Animals of one species can breed with others of the same species.
Territory – the area inhabited and defended by an animal or by a pair of animals.
Vertebrate – an animal with a skeleton and a well-developed brain; e.g. fishes, mammals.

Latin names

This is a list of the Latin names of all the aquarium fishes illustrated in this book. The first name beside each page number belongs to the fish at the top of the page, the second name belongs to the next fish shown and so on. The common (English) name may vary from country to country, but the Latin name stays the same.

Scorecard

The aquarium fishes on this scorecard are arranged in alphabetical order. When you spot a particular species, fill in the date next to its name. You can add up your score after a day out spotting.

	Score	Date seen		Score	Date seen
Acara, Blue	10		Catfish, Banjo	20	
American Flagfish	15		Catfish Bristlenose	10	
Angelfish (any)	5		Catfish, Electric	25	
Anostomus, Striped	15		Catfish, Glass	10	
Archerfish	25		Catfish, Upside-down	10	
Argentine Pearl Fish	15		Catfish, Whiptail	20	
Badis	15		Characin, Spraying	15	
Barb, Black Ruby	5		Characin, Swordtail	15	
Barb, Cherry	5		Chinese Algae Eater	10	
Barb, Golden	5		Cichlid, Convict	20	
Barb, Island	10		Cichlid, Eye-spot	15	
Barb, Rosy	5		Cichlid, Festive	10	
Barb, Tiger	5		Cichlid, Firemouth	15	
Barb, Tinfoil	10		Cichlid, Flag	10	
Beacon Fish	5		Cichlid, Jewel	10	
Blind Cave Fish	5		Cichlid, Keyhole	10	
Bloodfin	10		Cichlid, Nyasa Golden	15	
Blue Gularis	20		Cichlid, Zebra Nyasa	10	
Bumblebee Fish	15		Climbing Perch	15	
Butterfly Fish	20		Corydoras, Black Spotted	10	
Catfish, Albino	5		Corydoras, Bronze	5	

	Score	Date seen		Score	Date seen
Corydoras, Leopard	5		Guenther's Nothobranch	25	
Danio, Leopard	20		Guppy	5	
Danio, Pearl	10		Halfbeak	20	
Danio, Spotted	15		Harlequin Fish	5	
Danio, Zebra	5		Hatchetfish, Common	10	
Discus	5		Hatchetfish, Marbled	10	
Dragonfin	20		Headstander, Spotted	10	
Dwarf Cichlid, Borelli's	15		Jack Dempsey	15	
Dwarf Cichlid, Golden-eyed	10		Japanese Medaka	10	
Dwarf Cichlid, Yellow	20		Killi, Spanish	25	
Elephant Fish, Long-nosed	20		Killifish, Day's	15	
Epiplatys, Firemouth	20		Knifefish, Clown	20	
Flying Fox	15		Kribensis	5	
Foureyes	20		Leaf Fish	20	
Gambusia	20		Loach, Banded	10	
Glassfish, Indian	15		Loach, Clown	5	
Glassfish, Siamese	20		Loach, Coolie	5	
Golden Ear	15		Lyretail, Plumed	20	
Goldfish (any)	5		Minnow, Pike Top	20	
Gourami, Chocolate	20		Minnow, White Cloud Mountain	5	
Gourami, Dwarf	5		Molly	5	
Gourami, Giant	10		Molly, Black	5	
Gourami, Honey	5		Molly, Sailfin	10	
Gourami, Kissing	5		Mosquito Fish	20	
Gourami, Three-spot	5		Mouthbrooder, Dwarf Egyptian	10	

	Score	Date seen		Score	Date seen
Oscar	5		Siamese Fighting Fish	5	
Panchax, Playfair's	15		Sunfish, Black-banded	15	
Panchax, Striped	20		Sunfish, Dwarf	15	
Paradise Fish	10		Swordtail	5	
Paradise Fish, Comb-tailed	20		Tetra, Black-line	10	
Pencilfish, Dwarf	10		Tetra, Black Neon	10	
Pencilfish, Golden	10		Tetra, Black Phantom	10	
Pencilfish, Three-banded	15		Tetra, Buenos Aires	15	
Penguin Fish	5		Tetra, Cardinal	5	
Piranha (any)	20		Tetra, Congo	10	
Platy	5		Tetra, Diamond	15	
Pufferfish, Common	20		Tetra, Emperor	15	
Pufferfish, Green	25		Tetra, Flag	10	
Pufferfish Figure-eight	25		Tetra, Flame	10	
Rainbowfish, Australian	15		Tetra, Glass	15	
Rainbowfish, Celebes	20		Tetra, Glowlight	5	
Ram	10		Tetra, Griem's	15	
Rasbora, Elegant	10		Tetra, Jewel	10	
Rasbora, Pearly	15		Tetra, Lemon	10	
Rasbora, Scissortail	10		Tetra, Neon	5	
Rasbora, Spotted	10		Tetra, Red-nosed	10	
Rivulus, Cuban	20		Tetra, Red Phantom	20	
Rivulus, Golden-keeled	20		Tetra, Silver	15	
Shark, Red-fin	10		X-ray Fish	20	
Shark, Red-tailed Black	5				

Index